GOD ALWAYS KNEW

GOD ALWAYS KNEW

One Woman's Extraordinary Journey from
the Ashes of Self-Destruction
into the Beauty of a Surrendered Life.

Kerry Monroe

Jebaire Publishing
Snellville, GA

God Always Knew
Copyright©2011 Kerry Monroe
Published by Jebaire Publishing, LLC

All rights reserved. No part of this publication may be reproduced or transmitted in any form or by any means, electronic or mechanical, including photocopying and recording, or by any information storage and retrieval system, without written permission from the author.

All scripture quotations, unless otherwise indicated, are taken from the Holy Bible, New King James Version. Copyright © 1982 by Thomas Nelson, Inc. Used by permission. All rights reserved.

ISBN-13: 9780983854807
Library of Congress Control Number: 2011934892

Supervising Editor: Shannon Clark
Cover Design: Jebaire Publishing, LLC
Design/Editorial Assistant: Kerry Monroe

Visit Kerry Monroe's site at: www.kerrymonroe.com

Jebaire Publishing, LLC is an independent, non-denominational Christian book publisher. We are a free press and report to no outside groups. Our mission is to provide relevant Christian resources that both inspire and encourage our readers to pursue a meaningful relationship with God our Father through His son Jesus Christ.

Jebaire's website at: www.jebairepublishing.com

Printed in the United States

Dedication

To all the brave women whose lives have been an outstanding example to me of what it means to boldly "live out" God's foundational truth.

Contents

A Special Message
9

Preface
11

Acknowledgments
13

Can Anything Good Come from Nazareth?
17

Behind the Mask
25

Even in the Darkest Valley, God is There
33

God Restores
43

Deep Calls Out to Deep
53

Saying our Good-Byes
63

Grace for the Journey
73

Hope and a Future
85

Author Bio
91

Salvation Prayer
93

References
95

A Special Message

I would like to take a moment to thank the women who have impacted my life. These women (most I have never met) have exhibited exceptional courage and have been an example to me to not only proclaim, but also demonstrate that my freedom is in Christ alone. By the power of the Holy Spirit, they have fought against the lie of the enemy who desires us to live under the heavy garment of shame — attempting to hide what God has already removed and redeemed. The evidence of this lie is when a child of God continues to feel defiled and ashamed or chooses to be disobedient because they feel hopeless. But, these women, whether from Scripture or ones I have known personally, have in many ways invested into my life. These precious women have taught me how to share my testimony in a respectful and honorable way by reflecting the grace and truth of the Living God in my life.

This book is for every woman who still has that frightened little child inside of her and desires to be delivered from the ties of painful memories. I want to impart to you this simple truth: Once we learn to freely open our hearts and stop numbing our pain with the things that leave us spiritually bankrupt, God can and will enter in with His healing touch and bring about complete wholeness. With His help, we are able to face any kind of past abuse and rise above it. We can live a full, abundant life even after the unexpected trauma of death or disease. Most of all, each of us can be used as an instrument to serve the Lord no matter what our age, past, or marital status because the Lord draws us and reminds us to "Whom" we belong and how we can live in the light of His truth.

The story that you are about to read is a personal one. Writing this book was not the way I ever imagined serving the Lord, but I love Him, and He has invited me to lay down my life (my pride) and embark on a spirit-filled journey with Him. His love working through me gives grace to my new identity in Christ, so I desire to do whatever is in His will.

Embracing my freedom in Christ is a daily challenge, but I am determined to not let irrational fears, addictions, loneliness, or my feelings rule over me. Just as the Lord told Lazarus to take the grave clothes off and walk out in the freedom of his resurrection, I too have taken off the grave clothes called shame and secrets to bare witness of the miraculous and beautiful work Christ did for each of us on the cross.

God is Love and He has revealed Himself to me. I now live in a joyous peace with Him, and I invite you to receive the same tangible intimacy.

Preface

The reason I have chosen to write an autobiography called *God Always Knew* is because God has been gently peeling away the layers of my life so that I could see for myself what He knew was already there. With much patience He has encouraged me to look beneath the newly exposed layers to discover who I am in Christ. This has deepened my relationship with Him and allowed me to be a more useful and compassionate tool for His kingdom. I no longer fear my past.

2 Corinthians 1:3-4 says,

> [3] *Blessed be the God and Father of our Lord Jesus Christ, the Father of mercies and God of all comfort,* [4] *who comforts us in all our tribulation, that we may be able to comfort those who are in any trouble, with the comfort with which we ourselves are comforted by God.*

Comforting others is only possible when we give our wounds to the Lord and allow Him to heal them. Once healed, it then becomes our privilege and obligation to minister to others with healing words and great comfort. And that is what I hope this book can do for those who have struggled with past wounds. It is our "ministry of reconciliation" to share with others the kindness that the Lord has freely shown us. God will always take what was meant for evil and use it for His good… if we allow it. It is our daily choice.

Each chapter is divided into "stages" or "seasons" of my life. I didn't feel that it was necessary to give every dark detail of my past, but I did share many of them. This has been a time of peeling away those protective layers that kept me distant from God. I chose "other things/lesser things" to satisfy my true longing that could only be filled by Him. Surprisingly (although it has taken me years to believe), I have been unearthing His love for me layer by layer throughout the course of my life, starting back in 1958 in the city of Palm Springs.

As I look back over my life, I recognize that memories may be obscured and possibly one-sided. It is possible to share the same experience with others but be affected differently. I have made every attempt to record my memories to the best of my ability. I am sure in heaven my "view point"; my judgments of people, of myself, and even of my evaluation of my experiences will be enlarged to me. But for now, I can only rely on what is true to me.

Ultimately, this book is about taking the things of our past (good and bad) and like Paul stated in Phillipians 3:13-14, forgetting about them. We can so easily retreat and sink into discouragement by what and how the world (even from the church) perceives circumstances that we may be traveling through. There were times in my own past that I sunk into what seemed like a pit of quicksand. I not only struggled with my own delusions about what I was experiencing but also the perception of others. I didn't understand, then, that God had so much more prepared for me in heavenly realms. Now I see my past for what it is — a tool that has shaped me into the person I am today. While it's true that we can never truly forget our past until heaven, we can learn not to wallow in it, but rather, use it as a stepping stone to greater things. We do this in order to reach for the goal of the prize of the higher calling of God in Christ Jesus.

Wisdom has taught me over the years that just because a family looks healthy on the outside (out in public), does not mean that behind closed doors it is a safe place. We can learn something from the negative experiences of our past and rise above them. We don't have to understand it, but if we've been hurt, we must learn to receive and/or give forgiveness. This necessary act frees us to depend more upon the Lord and be used to help others in their journey.

This is my story. . .

Acknowledgments

I am so very thankful God directed me to a Bible-based church where truth and grace are demonstrated and the whole council of God's Word is preached. Calvary Chapel Eastside is my home church where I am loved; where my faith has been challenged, and where I have been allowed to grow in maturity as I daily live for Jesus Christ.

Shannon, my editor and friend, thank you. I have appreciated your sensitivity to those fears that I have had to lay down with the writing of this book. You have shared your sweet spirit of encouragement knowing how difficult each of these subjects were to face —as well as write about. You handled each one gently, giving me insight like, "He created you for this very specific purpose – your purpose defines you not your past." You took a diamond in the rough (this book) and with your heavenly gift and craftsman's tool, you shaped, chiseled, and polish it to make it shine for God's glory. Best of all, we have become dear and faithful friends.

Kim, you were the first person who encouraged me to tell my story in book form, not for any other reason but to show the wonders of God's redeeming grace. Thank you for seeing and believing in me more than I could see in myself. Your love is a steady anchor, and your gift of encouragement is a reminder of the God-given gift we all can give to others.

God has blessed me with many wonderful friends and a dear sister-in-law to which I am thankful and humbled by their love. Linda, Gail, Laurie, Margaret, Lin, Shelly, Lou, Leslie and Beth, thank you for being apart of my daily life and the millions of ways you have shown me great love. You make my heart so full and remind me of the verse in Ecclesiastes that says a three strand cord is not easily broken. Through the years, we have grown together, been challenged by our circumstances, and proven that the depth of friendships will out last anything that comes our way.

I have so many more dear friends who know they are also loved and appreciated.

To my precious children: Brenden, Marlana, Micah. You have surprised me with just how far reaching a mother's love can embrace each of her children. Our home has been a place where comfort and acceptance are always found. I pray that your daddy's and my love for you has been the glue that will always bind us together closely as a family. Although we've had to battle in the trenches of sorrow and loss, through Christ we have risen to now stand on the mountain top. I've learned that although human love is imperfect, where God's love, grace and forgiveness rules, a family can forge forward and become a thing of beauty. May you always remember me as just a simple woman whose main desire was to always follow hard after Jesus. And with the purest act of love I can have for you, I surrender each of you to the Lord. For truly, I have been an earthly vessel of His love and you each belong to Him.

To Jim my husband: I shall carry my love, devotion, and sweet words for you forever in my heart. You seemed to bring out the best in me. From the beginning you brought new life and deep love into my world, and I returned that love 'til that last breath you took upon this earth. Accepting your death has been my greatest struggle. I miss you daily. I will be your wife for all eternity . . . wait for me.

The greatest thing I have ever done in my life is recognize my desperate need for my Savior and surrendering my heart to Him. I am a sinner saved by grace. Thank you Jesus for counting the cost and dying that I might live. May it be my life's devotion and purpose to share with others that this Good News is for them also!

IN CHRIST, WE ARE....

Delivered from death
Renewed after redemption
Moved over mercy
Transformed through truth
Strengthened having suffered
Faced with forgiveness
Called for compassion
Guided towards grace
Freed in faith
Held by hope...

And liberated to love

~~~

Simple blessings,
K.M.

God Always Knew

1

Can Anything Good Come From Nazareth?

Is anyone really born in Palm Springs California? I think I have heard that question countless times in my 50 years. Gee, it kind of reminds me of the scripture: "Can anything good come from of Nazareth?" (John 1:46). Just to be clear, in 1958 many babies were born in the city of Palm Springs California, and I was among that baby count.

Keeping Up Appearances

My family looked the part. My dad was a big, tall, movie star-handsome fella, and my mother was a tiny and adorable beauty. My sister and I were towhead blonde little girls. It was the mid 50's, and we were living in a dream house in the best part of town. My father owned his own real estate brokerage company selling homes to the wealthy stars of Hollywood who used Palm Springs as their getaway place. We were what the world would size up as the "perfect" looking family.

My mother was a stay-at-home mom, something that was not unusual back then; however, this convenience was only for my father's benefit, so he could control her every move. My father came home everyday from work during lunch time to eat a bologna sandwich and check in—to assess and dominate. It was all about control. My mother was not allowed to go anywhere without my father's permission, and he watched her closely to make sure. It is a frightening thing to watch a man charm his way into the hearts of others, knowing how quickly that could turn out of control once inside the privacy of the home. The only memory I have as a child (my sister and mother may have additional memories), of him losing control out in public, was one afternoon when he drove by the outdoor tennis courts at the neighborhood park and "caught" my mother playing tennis with a girlfriend. Without reservation, he simply got out of his car from where he had been spying on her and dragged her by her hair taking her off the courts. I followed behind with silent tears because even at the tender age of five years old, I knew better than to show protest and make noise. Punishment could come in the form of either the silent treatment for several weeks with only the "evil-eye-stare" (we called it "the look") or the other form of punishment would be the brunt of an alcoholic rage. Of course, the rage would be over quicker, but it was always more terrorizing. To this day, I can't say what was easier to live through.

The day we left my father and Palm Springs was as frightening and dramatic as a good daytime soap opera. Earlier that day, my father found our packed bags which indicated our escape plans. He drove my mother out to the desert and dumped the bags, leaving her out there to walk back alone. When he returned home, he disassembled her car making it impossible to drive us away. I am not sure how many hours went by, but my next memory was one of being huddled together with my mother and sister behind the locked door of my parent's bedroom. In a fit of rage my father pounded on the door with his fist until he eventually broke it down. Afterward, we were sent to our rooms where we could safely hide under our bed covers and attempt to block out the angry voices. I don't know what he did to my mother that night. She never shared that with us.

Just before sunrise the next morning, I was awakened by my mother's whisper telling me to get dressed because we were leaving daddy. I thought we were playing a game but I would soon find out that we were not. We left Palm Springs early that morning on bicycles with no luggage. My frightened mother and her two wide-eyed children rode under the protection of the dark morning sky (right through downtown) until we arrived to my mother's friend's home.

She kept us hidden in some dark place until we could safely escape to a bus stop. My last childhood memory in Palm Springs was that of my father's footsteps in this house of my mother's friend. We all were frozen in fear by the screaming voice of my father saying he knew we were there and that this woman was in on it too.

The Road to Shame

It's crazy to admit that I have no memory of my mother's personality or outward affection toward her two children in those early years. I'm not saying this to accuse her. It's just the way things were. Of course she had affection for us. She could have just left us there and only freed herself. As an adult I now realize she must have done her best in those circumstances and gave only what she had to give. I'm sure living through that mess must have changed her deeply. It surely changed me.

I also wonder what could have happened in my own father's life that would manifest itself in this kind of behavior. Did his own parents abuse him, and he just couldn't break the cycle? What kind of pain did he encounter to bring out this pattern that continued and got terribly worse as the years went on? (I would later receive firsthand knowledge of the brutal force behind his intensity.)

Without a personal relationship with Jesus Christ and a willingness to carry His love in us, I fear none of us are exempt from walking and behaving in a self-destructive manner—resorting to our most basic primal behaviors. It is amazing how low a person can go when they live in anarchy (self-rule and not living under the power of the Holy Spirit). I know I wallowed in my own base passions for quite some time.

When we really look deeply within ourselves, don't we all desire control in some way? Maybe we go about it in what we surmise as a "better way", but our better way can turn into the manipulation of others based on our selfish desires. If we discover this to be true about ourselves (though this painful pattern of behavior is difficult to recognize in oneself), we must ask the Lord for forgiveness and allow Him to change us.

I have had to face the consequences of my own sins and recognize that I need my Savior's redemption. I believe that it's important to share the *when* and *how* my layers of protection/shame began, so that you can see what it took to finally allow God to peel them away and heal my heart. It has been a painful process that I have only in the last 15 years been able to feel ready enough to begin. I can only hope that this transparency with you will either help you to face your own layers or at the very least not be so judgmental of others.

Remember this: The enemy wants us to continue to live in shame and secrecy so that he is not exposed as the liar he is. This is one of the reasons why so many of us keep our past experiences a secret. Even now while writing this I know I am under attack from the enemy. He doesn't want us to share our stories of redemption. The enemy of our soul does not want me to tell you of the freedom we have as a child of God, the Most High.

Reflections

I believe that I developed my innermost layer of shame during my childhood. It became my protective barrier to the outside world. These layers protected me from the deep seated pain I carried. I don't believe I'll ever understand the depth of the hole in my little heart or the way I would learn to self-protect in order to shield myself from future pain. I never called out to the Lord for help in those early years. The Lord Jesus was not someone I knew existed and yet, I now see just how He was protecting me all along. This is His nature.

While there are many dark memories in my past that would crowd out any sense of childhood normalcy that I might attempt to grasp, there were some sweet and precious moments that I will always hold close to my heart. I remember fondly happier times spent swimming in our backyard pool to keep cool or the click-clack of my shiny black tap shoes. Wet puppy dog kisses, tangerines picked right off our trees, and walking to school with my older sister dressed in matching clothes are some of the sweetest moments that I hold close to me. I've learned to search for the good in all things and not allow the pain of my soul to get out of balance. Twisted scars have a way of hovering around and eclipsing the good times that occur (even in the madness). It's only been in the last few years as I've studied what experts have to say (see References) that I've begun to understand just how toxic negative experiences can be on even our own recall of childhood memories — especially those born out of sexual abuse. Just like many other adults who have traveled a similar road, I have huge gaps, chunks of time just gone. Most of my memories are like bits of short clips that pop into my head— even some inappropriate situations with my father. I can't seem to truly grasp all of it, so I continue to trust in God's ability to walk with me down whatever memory lane is pertinent to my healing. I ask Him to awaken whatever I've allowed to die as a way of coping. If it does not all return fully, then when I take my last breath here on earth and enter into the presence of my Savior, that either all the past times will be revealed and understood or totally wiped clear. No matter which of these turns out to be true, I don't think I'll really care by then.

Some of you reading this now have your own memories of verbal or physical abuse and that has been the reason for your layers too. Haunting memories are pushed so far down that they seem hidden to you, but God would ask you to allow His Spirit to do the healing work. This work will allow the barriers to crumble down, soften your heart and prepare you for the healing that is yours as His child. Will you invite Him in? He's waiting for you.

As I close this chapter and before beginning a new one, I'd like to share Psalm 91. It so beautifully displays the layers of love our God has for us. I personally claim this psalm for my life: *His wings covered and gave me refuge; His angels stood charge over me. I learned to not be afraid of the night, and sorrow has not kept me a prisoner.* Jesus became my trusted Salvation and Deliverer!

<u>Psalm 91</u>:

He, who dwells in the secret place of the Most High, shall abide under the shadow of the Almighty. I will say of the Lord, "He is my refuge and my fortress; My God, in Him I will trust." Surely He shall deliver you from the snare of the fowler and from the perilous pestilence. He shall cover you with His feathers, and under His wings you shall take refuge; His truth shall be your shield and buckler. You shall not be afraid of the terror by night, nor of the arrow that flies by day, nor of the pestilence that walks in darkness, nor of the destruction that lays waste at noonday. A thousand may fall at your side, and ten thousand at your right hand; but it shall not come near you. Only with your eyes shall you look, and see the reward of the wicked. Because you have made the Lord who is my refuge even the Most High, your dwelling place, no evil shall befall you, nor shall any plague come near your dwelling; For He shall give His angels charge over you, to keep you in all your ways. In their hands they shall bear you up, lest you dash your foot against a stone. You shall tread upon the lion and the cobra, the young lion and the serpent you shall trample underfoot. "Because he has set his love upon Me, therefore, I will deliver him; I will set him upon high, because he has known My name, He shall call upon Me, and I will answer him; I will be with him in trouble; I will deliver him and honor him. With long life I will satisfy him, and show him My salvation.

    Does this Psalm speak to your heart? Is there a time where you need to thank the Lord for His deliverance in your life? Does the "little child" in you need to learn to trust again? Give God your thoughts: __

_____
_____
_____
_____
_____
_____
_____
_____
_____
_____
_____

EVEN BEFORE

Before Your hands selected and fixed into place each
and every star in the Heavens to glimmer
throughout the darkened skies—
Your thought was for me.

Before Your hands defined and marked off the boarders
of the ocean waters or curved the river's edge—
Your heart possessed a love for me.

From the very bottom depths of the sea; rugged canyon walls,
from the dark interior of hidden caves, or to the highest exposed mountain top and far beyond any visible sky—
Your eye was on me.

Before Your hands set and planted each tree
within the prepared ground, or generously scattered
the wildflowers from far and near---
Your delight was for me.

Even before Your hands fashioned and formed creation, or
spoke the words, "Let Us make man in Our likeness",
even before Your Spirit breath gave life —
Your mission and purpose was always for me.

O Lord, before I ever question Your love for me,
or my value to You, help me to remember and
claim these truths I possess as a
child of Yours!

~~~

Simple Blessings
K.M.

God Always Knew

2

Behind the Mask

The three of us were all trying to adapt to our new life in a new city. Friends needed to be made at our new school and our mother had to step into the role of head of the household and primary provider. Leaving everything behind and starting over with two small children must have been frightening and difficult for her (I am so very sorry that I never told her how brave she must have been). Despite the drastic changes, she got a job making and selling tennis dresses and flourished. She must have felt so proud to survive.

As I got older, however, the layers of secrecy began to thicken around my heart, stumping the growth of my soul. During a visit from our paternal grandfather (our first time ever meeting him), my mother found out that he was Jewish. She'd always thought that our father's family name was German. Not too long after that visit she changed our last name and cautioned us to never speak about our bloodline that she felt was tainted (more shame to hide and more rejection felt). What does an 8 or 9-year-old, with no prior religious background, even know about being Jewish? I only knew that I was being told that something else was wrong with me and that I must hide that truth from others. Unlike Esther (from the Old Testament), I was not being told to hide my Jewish bloodline out of safety. I was told to hide it out of shame. *Oh, Father in Heaven, thank you for your forgiveness.*

When my father found out we'd changed our last name to my mother's maiden name, he stopped making childcare payments. My mother was often in court battling my father for the money, so my sister and I often had to speak to the judge in a courtroom.

> *Why is transaprency so difficult?*
>
> *Why are we so afraid of what others will think about us? Do we worry that they'll say negative things behind our backs, or perhaps, that they'll judge us when they find out who we *really* are? We hold back truths thinking that it will protect us from the perceived pain of revealing our faults. We then convince ourselves that hiding things won't matter much, but it does. We must remember that in God's economy, placing man's opinion above the thoughts God is a sin.*
>
> *God desires that we not only stand bare before Him, but also the world around us. He sent His Son to die for the world's sins (our sins) and bridge the gap to Him. Jesus hung on the cross naked for all to behold, yet, in essence, every time we try to "save face" before others, we are shamefully covering the redemptive work of the blood that Jesus shed on the cross for us. Isn't this what Adam and Eve did when they hid their nakedness?*
>
> *What is God encouraging you to share about your life with someone in need today? Remember, no one's opinion is greater than God's unveiled truth, so don't be ashamed of where you've been. It's the redemptive work of Christ within our hearts and in our lives that is the true indication of our worth.*

The huge courtroom and judge always scared me. It wasn't long before I began to withdraw. It is strange how quickly we can adjust to a world of secrecy even at a young age. When someone approaches you with questions about your past or family, you learn to dodge the subject. It wasn't that difficult, and with practice I had gotten really good at it.

At the same time that I began grappling with my own insecurities, my mother began to thrive in her newly found freedom. Of course she would! She was a beautiful woman who had been treated badly. She bought flashier clothes, wore more makeup, and started dating. To be fair, it was the late 60's and clothing styles had drastically changed. She was flourishing , but as a young child, I became jealous. I hated that she would leave us at home and go out at night with strange men. I hated that she acted silly and flirtatious toward them. I so desperately wanted to be a part of that affection. I wanted to see her eyes light up for me the way they did for those men. It all seems so silly to me now that I'm an adult. As a woman I can understand her need and desire to want to find a husband to help her and love her. More importantly, I realize that the need for a man's affection was a separate emotion that had nothing to do with my mother's ability to show us affection. But at the time, I just loved spending time with her, like on our nights when we would sit all together and watch the TV show "Laugh In". I guess I wanted all of her attention.

Soon enough my mother did find herself a second husband, and for awhile things felt more settled in our home. He was very pleasant in the beginning and kind to my sister and I. But again, alcohol brought out the worst and in a few years, things began to change.

A Chance Meeting

My best friend during this time invited me to go to a youth group program at a local nondenominational church. I loved youth group. There was something about the experience and the people that was so inviting to my wounded soul, and I felt safe under their watchful care. We both lied to our parents about our participation. My friend's reasons were because her parents were Roman Catholic and they would not approve. My reason was that my mother didn't like our friendship because she was Italian (1st generation American).

One night the group went on an outing to our local movie theater to watch an outreach movie put on by the Billy Graham Association. I heard God's call that night. He was drawing me to Himself and I could feel and taste my desperate need to be loved by Him. The alter call was made by someone in the front of the movie theater, and I responded by walking up. Shaking with excitement, I received Jesus Christ into my heart and as my personal Savior. I never wanted to leave that night. It was my mountain top experience. I wanted to keep the joy, peace, and thrill of the experience with me as long as possible. Admittedly, I really didn't understand how the whole religious thing worked. In my naiveté, I assumed that anyone who felt the same zeal for Jesus that I did would have to become a nun (like in the TV movies). And I was willing.

The Lord set my soul on fire for Him that day. When I opened myself up to Him and His Spirit, He touched the core of my heart and penetrated the deepest layers of my soul. His love can do that. He can speak life even into those areas of my past that have been locked away and left to die. Is the broken child inside of you still screaming silently to be noticed, loved and appreciated? What you are seeking may never come from those who should have given it to you freely, but God desires to be your Abba Father and to kiss away the hurting places. Take His hand, and He will walk alongside you and speak encouraging words to your soul.

Despite the bad times, God was always there and is still there to mend the broken pieces. As I end this chapter, I'd like to share another Psalm with you. Psalm 63 reminds me that no matter how deep the layers of my life go, He will never leave me. I sought the Lord and thirsted for His loving kindness and He redeemed me and washed me clean. He does more than just uphold each of us; He gives "fatness" to our soul. In hard times we must remember His goodness.

Psalm 63

Oh God, You are my God; early will I seek You; my soul thirsts for You; my flesh longs for You in a dry and thirsty land where there is no water. So I have looked for You in the sanctuary to see Your power and Your glory. Because Your loving kindness is better than life, my lips shall praise

You. Thus I will bless You while I live; I will lift up my hands in Your name. My soul shall be satisfied as with marrow and fatness, and my mouth shall praise You with joyful lips. When I remember You on my bed, I meditate on You in the night watches. Because You have been my help, therefore in the shadow of Your wings I will rejoice. My soul follows close behind You; Your right hand upholds me. But those who seek my life, to destroy it, shall go into the lower parts of the earth. They shall fall by the sword; they shall be a portion for jackals. But the king shall rejoice in God; everyone who swears by Him shall glory; but the mouth of those who speak lies shall be stopped.

Do you need "fatness" that only the Lord can provide? Are you feeling hungry and thirsty for God's presence? Maybe it's time to seek Him in the sanctuary of His presence and invite Him into your heart? Give Jesus the prayer of your heart.

_____
_____
_____
_____
_____
_____
_____
_____
_____
_____
_____

God Always Knew

MY CHILD

Child, sweet child of Mine~
I see your constant struggles
and hear the silent cry of your heart,
I want you to know that you may rest in Me-
for I'm the Lord God… I AM.
I am your Healer, your Help and the eternal Hope.

My child, the many tears that fall~
I collect and tenderly treasure them all.
That soiled stain is cleansed and forever removed,
and I want you to know that you are pure in Me-
for I'm the Lord God… I AM.
I am your Redeemer, your Reward and the unmovable Rock.

Oh child, sweet child of Mine~
Allow Me to burn away those shadows,
and speak truth to your soul.
I loose the heavy shackles that chain you down,
and set you free in Me-
For I'm the Lord God…I AM.
I am your Protector, your Portion, and the Divine Promise.

Trust always in Me my child,
Even in the hardest and darkest of times, for your life matters
to Me~
then be strengthened by how My love has engraved you
forever in the palm of My hands.
I'm the Lord God… I AM

~~~

Simple Blessings
K.M.

God Always Knew

3

Even In The Darkest Valley God Is There

The heartbreaking truth is that the newly found exuberance that I had for Jesus—to follow Him at any cost—was not shared at home. No Jesus freaks allowed. The Billy Graham Association had given each of us who received Jesus Christ a New Testament Bible to read. My mother took my Bible away and forbade me to attend youth group. This was a devastating blow to me as a new Christian. As a babe in Christ, I needed to feed on God's Word and be encouraged in His principles. In this absence, I drifted away from my "first love". Confusion set in and in error, I began to believe that God had abandoned me. Of course, this was a lie from Satan, but I didn't understand his cunning ways, and so I believed him. Have you ever doubted God's love for you? The enemy of our soul will try to confuse us, but we can trust that once we have asked Jesus Christ into our hearts, nothing can snatch us away!

In the Valley

As I got older, I found that I was a natural at playing tennis. I was able to play for hours after school and compete in tournaments on the weekends. It was a great outlet and gave me confidence. My mother and "step father" (although I was never adopted by him) belonged to a tennis/golf club. This provided me the privilege of taking lessons, and I was able to play on the best courts. I was happiest when playing. I felt strong and in more control on those tennis courts. It was as if I was someone else—someone I liked better. I continued to thrive in the sport, even playing for my high school's tennis team, but I still felt so lost. Masks are so easy to put on and wear, but my inside soul knew what I was missing.

During this time of spiritual upheaval, a boy from my school was in an accident and died. Several of the students went to his celebration/memorial service. While attending it myself, I was approached by one of our school's football players to go on a ride in his VW van. I was so thrilled to be asked (even noticed) by this popular boy, I quickly agreed without thinking the situation out. If I'd only known what was really on his mind.

The fact that I was raped and sodomized is unthinkable, but to have it happen at a tender and innocent age is life changing. I was only 15 years old. After he was finished with me, he dropped me back off at the home where the celebration was still under way.

Today, I have more questions than I have answers. Was it my demeanor that made me seem like "easy pickin's"? And after all these years it is unimaginable to me that I never told anyone. Why? Didn't I know that he could do this to some other girl, and I had the power to expose him? Sadly, none of those thoughts came to mind back then. I just took what happened and buried it deeply. I had to, because I saw him everyday at school. It wasn't until about 15 years later that I decided to share what had happened, and that was only to my husband, and after five years into our marriage.

A Slippery Slope

Within a year after the rape, my mother's marriage began to fall apart. The rebellion in me was in full force. My grades started dropping as I spent more time skipping school than staying in. There were late nights out, sleeping around with boys, heavy drug use/drinking, and the abortion my mother helped me get because I didn't want the inconvenience. Although I chose to allow the removal of God's creation from my body, I just couldn't get past what I'd done. Not long after the abortion, I took a small knife to the back of my wrists and cut them. I didn't really want to die, I didn't cut that deeply. It was a cry for help. I think I just wanted attention. I was spiraling out of control and at the end of my ability to cope. I was taken to the hospital and they sewed me up. The experience was put in another "file cabinet" in my head where I closed it and clicked it shut to never think about it again.

My years of rebellion finally came to a head when I ran away from home. A few weeks later, I was caught by the police and brought to juvenile hall where I stayed for one week. I caused so much anguish and heartache to my mother for that week I was gone. My mother thought the incarceration would be a good lesson for me. She was right; it was a very good lesson. Being locked in that place with its cold, grey walls and sounds of heavy doors shutting and locking was very frightening *and good place* to do a lot of thinking.

I am a mother now and cannot imagine what kind of pain my mother endured not knowing where her youngest daughter was. It was such a selfish act on my part. It's hard to admit the abusive things we do to ourselves and others. Why do we think that when we bury the bad things that happen to us, they won't affect our soul?

A Last Resort

When I was released from juvenile hall, my packed bags were waiting for me outside by the car. My mother and sister drove me directly to Palm Springs to live with my father, hoping I'd learn an even greater lesson. I know that my mother would have never put me in harm's way. How could she have known that my father had gotten so out of control. The severe beatings that I endured at his hand are difficult to discuss even today. I was a slender 5'5" 17- year- old. He was big and strong at 6'4" and towered over me. No longer able to control his temper, the anger continued to build inside of him. It made no difference if it was inside or outside the home. His alcohol addiction was affecting his mind, his business, and his relationships (failed marriages). He forced me to go to the bar with him while he drank. My father loved to laugh about how he had at one time put a "hit" out on my mother. I don't know if that is true or just crazy talk. I just tried to keep up with my homework because I still needed to go to school in the morning. *I missed so much school during my high school years that I'm still very sensitive today about my lack of education.* Thankfully, after some time spent begging my mother to take me back, my sister came and got me. I kept my word and caused no more trouble.

On My Own

Within a few months after graduating from high school, I went to work for a commercial airline out of Houston, Texas as a flight attendant. I loved to fly and travel, and I was good at my job. My new career gave me a sense of freedom that I'd never felt before and I succumbed to the intoxication of being on my own. Again, I chose badly and began to abuse what I had.

The next 8 years are a blur of self-abuse and rebellion against God. He gives us the free choice to either be controlled by His Spirit or by our flesh and I was choosing my flesh. The pain of my past had wrapped itself so tightly around me that I was suffocating. I'd fallen into Satan's trap, and spiritual freedom no longer mattered to me. He enticed me into believing that empty and harmful things would fill the void that I felt in my soul, but this was a lie. Only God's amazing redeeming love can fill us.

God spoke in Jeremiah 2:13,

> *For My people have committed two evils, they have forsaken Me, the fountain of living waters, and hewn themselves cisterns—broken cisterns that can hold no water.*

I was that person. I was finding comfort in other things instead of going to the Lover of my soul. I filled myself with the world's temptations—drugs that only numbed for awhile; parties that ended and left me lonely again; sex that could never fill the longing that I had for true companionship; and spending money that only filled my closet but not my soul. It is all counterfeit and not what God has for us.

    Admittedly, at the time I loved the power. I loved the control I felt I had over men. I used my charm and outward beauty for my own selfishness and foolish pride. I was good at being flirtatious. It became an addiction in the worst of ways. I had a job that allowed me to fly to different states and to different countries, so I was giving myself to men in all those exotic places. I felt like an empty shell, not realizing that I was a child of the Most High God and that my value could only be found in Jesus Christ. Oh, how I would have saved myself so much extra grief, if only I had known that truth.

    The consequences of living outside of God's will can become one of the hardest things to endure. There was another pregnancy, and another abortion followed. Then while traveling in Mexico and "living it up", I was given a date rape drug in a night club and taken to a man's home somewhere up on a hill in Puerto Vallarta where I was raped again. My memory of that night is fuzzy, but I will never forget the next morning. I didn't know where I was or how to get back to my hotel. All I wanted to do was shower away the filth. I felt so much shame. I hated who I'd become and convinced myself that this time I deserved what happened to me. My life was a mess, and I was tired of all the chaos.

    Similar to the nation of Israel in Old Testament times, I also had a problem with idolatry. Just as their rebellion led them into captivity, so had mine. I believe that God gave me over to my selfish ways so that I could be sickened by it and cured. I needed that wake up call. I needed to face my own sin, claim it, and be accountable for it. I needed to see the snare the enemy kept using to draw me into the same sins. I needed Christ back in my life. I began to think about how I felt once before when I was younger and had a small faith in Him. I started to pray and become curious about Him again. Still I wondered if I had gone too far for Him to forgive me. I didn't realize at the time that we have a God of many chances. His forgiveness washes away the stain of our poor choices. If we receive nothing else from Him in this life, His amazing redeeming love is plenty.

A New Heart

I began checking out churches that met on Saturday nights, so that I could hit the bar and dance clubs afterwards. I'd sleep off the night on Sunday mornings. Even then, the Holy Spirit was wooing me ever so gently. No matter how far away we walk from the Lord, His arms are never too short to gather us back into His loving care. No matter who has rejected us or abandoned us, God will never leave us. This is His promise to us and he does not lie! (Hebrews 6:18; Titus 1:2; Malachi 3:6; Numbers 23:19) You can stand on those scriptures. You can stand on that truth. Share this hope with others who might have a prodigal child, or receive this truth for yourself and be blessed!

Also remember that we cannot blame anyone else for our choices. Our decisions belong to us; however, we can allow God to pierce through the walls of self-destruction to reveal His goodness. When I held myself accountable for my actions and surrendered my will, God came into my heart and showed Himself to me. It was His grace and love that gave me the desire to repent and go a different way. . . His way. I wish I could say that it was one particular day or that it happened overnight, but I still stumbled in my Christian walk. Yet, the Lord patiently guided my steps back to His path. What a good and gracious God we have! How can I judge others or withhold my forgiveness when God did not hold back His Son for my soul?

I have never turned back from that time on. I have set my heart to be the Lord's. I am a follower of Jesus Christ. God was gracious with me, and cleansed me and justified me by His blood, and He'll do the same thing for you. I now have a clean heart and His Spirit never leaves me.

PSALM 51

Have mercy upon me, O God, according to Your lovingkindness; according to the multitude of Your tender mercies, blot out my transgressions. Wash me thoroughly from my iniquity, and cleanse me from my sin. For I acknowledge my transgressions, and my sin is always before me. Against You, You only, have I sinned, and done this evil in Your sight—that You may be found just when You speak, and blameless when You judge. Behold, I was brought forth in iniquity, and in sin my mother conceived me. Behold, You desire truth in the inward parts, and in the hidden part You will make me to know wisdom. Purge me with hyssop, and I shall be clean; wash me, and I shall be whiter than snow.Make me hear joy and gladness that the bones You have broken may rejoice. Hide Your face from my sins, and blot out all my iniquities. Create in me a clean heart, O God, and renew a steadfast spirit within me. Do not cast me away from Your presence, and do not take Your Holy Spirit from me. Restore to me the joy of Your salvation, and uphold me by Your generous Spirit. Then I will teach transgressors Your ways, and sinners shall be converted to You. Deliver me from the guilt of bloodshed, O God, the God of my salvation, and my tongue shall sing aloud of Your righteousness. O Lord, open my lips, and my mouth shall show forth Your praise. For You do not desire sacrifice, or else I would give it; You do not delight in burnt offering. The sacrifices of God are a broken spirit, a broken and a contrite heart—these, O God, You will not despise. Do good in Your good pleasure to Zion; build the walls of Jerusalem. Then You shall be pleased with the sacrifices of righteousness, with burnt offering and whole burnt offering; Then they shall offer bulls on Your altar.

Does the enemy keep bringing up your past to you and making you feel unlovable? It's because you remind him of the work Jesus did on the cross—chains have been broken. You might have a past, but Christ died for that. You are new in Jesus and a child of the Most High God. Live in that victory every day! Ask the Lord for a daily reminder of who you are in Him. _____
_____
_____

God Always Knew

Breath of Heaven

You are the Voice of Heaven, who speaks truth into the awaiting hearts of those of us who are truly desiring grace from above to rain down and melt away the hardened place of pride that we have the tendency to cling to and even feast upon.

Oh, Breath of Heaven who restores back to life from the grave of those neglected areas of our own soul, and with just one touch from You, brings about healing to our wounds and comfort to our afflictions - then releases our hearts to beat again with a Heavenly rhythm.

Precious Holy Oil of Heaven who searches and finds the hidden and fills the empty with Your Spirit of gladness, Your Spirit flows thoughout so that it flourishes our lives with Divine joy in You.

Oh, clear away all shadows and shine brightly as You guide us in this life journey, so that we may know the pure glory of You...You God, Who was, and is, and always will be the Light of Heaven.

~~~

Simple Blessings
K.M.

God Always Knew

4

God Restores

So I will restore to you the years that the swarming locust has eaten, the crawling locust, and the consuming locust, and the chewing locust, my great army which I sent among you.

-Joel 2:25 (NKJV)

God's Word is true. I willingly give witness to the fact that He will restore the years that the locust have eaten. Although more painful times would come, I'd soon discover that I wasn't alone. I could now face challenges in the power and strength of Jesus Christ which makes a huge difference. When you're walking with God and being surrendered to the work of the Holy Spirit you can ride the waves of trouble without being crushed by them.

New Beginnings

The day I met my future husband my whole world changed. I knew the moment I met Jim that I would long to know him forever. I couldn't exactly explain why… I just knew. There was a special quality about him that I found comforting. I knew it would be safe to love him. And oh, how he loved me! I was 26 years old and he was ten years older. I think it was the first time I felt loved.

We were married within 3 months and had many obstacles stacked against us. But, against all odds—past baggage, different upbringings, different financial and ethnic background . . . our marriage worked. It wasn't perfect, of course (none are), but my husband always reminded me that Christ was in our marriage and we couldn't "quit Christ", dishonor Him, or stay mad at each other. My husband had been raised in the church by godly parents and though he may have tested the waters of rebellion as a young man himself, he had a deep faith in his Lord, God. Jim taught me how to love by example.

Tragically, my mother just couldn't get past the color of my husband's skin, so she disowned me. Truthfully, I always thought that she would come around. I sent letters to her hoping to soften her heart. But sadly, she began returning them unopened, so I stopped sending them. Begging her for a relationship became too painful. It was such a terrible loss for us all. She never got to know our amazing kids or the love of my life. My family lost the chance to know my mother as a mother-in-law and as a grandma. And I lost my relationship with my own mother. It's a sadness that I carried with me throughout my marriage and still today. I did hear that she re-married two more times. I hope she finally found someone to truly love her.

Baby Steps

My first son, Brenden, was born in 1984 (on my husband's 36th birthday). Watching Jim hold his first child in the palm of his big strong hands melted my heart. If there was a way to give more of my heart to someone, I did that day. I gave my heart fully to both my precious child and husband. All that the 'locust' took from me was now a distant memory.

To be honest, I was a bit afraid of what kind of mother I would be. I wasn't sure if I carried a "violent gene" like my father or if I would just be cold and aloof to my baby. I believe that there are cycles of poor coping patterns, bad judgments and habits, but I also know that God is all about breaking dead and hurtful cycles and doing a new thing in a person's life (1 Corinthians 5:17). He says each soul is mine in Ezekiel 18:4. I am not my father, I am not my mother, but I am a child of the Most High God (made in His image).

A Daddy's Girl

I often think about not having a good example of what a father's love should feel like. Even today, when I'm invited to participate in other family gatherings, I often sit in silence lost in thoughts that swirl in my head like, "What would this feel like, to grow up knowing this kind of love, this kind of family connection, smothered with the richness of this heritage?" I don't permit myself to tarry there long, it can torture a person and drag them deep into a pool of self-pity.

Instead of staying in the pit of jealousy or resentment because of what I did not have, I've learned to lift my eyes to Jesus and praise Him for the blessings of others while giving Him my ache knowing He has already redeemed it. I believe that this has permitted me to minister to others with greater compassion.

Our Heavenly Father's love is the purest and most satisfying of all. It is through His loving embrace that I have learned what it truly means to be a "Daddy's Girl". I look forward to entering the Kingdom of heaven where I will be a part of THE largest family connection ever!

I soon found out that our baby boy would bring out the best in me. Even his endearing smile made my life feel more complete. It was a precious time. My heart was full of joy and healing slowly. I was learning what it meant to have a healthy family. My faith was growing in the Lord, and His love was restoring us.

Old Memories

My husband, son, and I were living in the bay area of Northern California and doing so well as a sweet little family. One night we got a surprise knock at our door by the local police to inform me that my father had committed suicide. This was a difficult shock to face. I immediately flew back to Palm Springs to take care of his remaining business and burial. My father never left a note of explanation, an apology, let alone a note of some kind of last loving words to his children. He only left instructions for the town paper's obituaries.

It was hard to walk back through that house and see the old blood stains in my bedroom from past beatings. Those memories made me physically ill. Then, to stand in the master bedroom where I could picture us all huddled together, knowing that this was the same room my father took a gun to his own head and ended his life, made me sick on so many different levels. Does it sound harsh when I admit that I am glad to have that chapter of my life over and the page turned? Because I've chosen to walk in forgiveness and let God handle the pain of my past, I am now free. The only feelings I carry now are of sadness because my father never found peace in his life, and I never got to know what a loving, caring earthly father relationship feels like. I don't know if he ever gave his heart to Jesus before he died. I can only hope that he did. Satan is a liar and a robber, and if we choose it, he will steal our soul.

After dealing with my dad's remains, I went back home to my own family. I could see where God was restoring my life, and I was thankful; but I was still keeping my past completely guarded. Only my husband knew my story. No one else knew about my dad, my rape or my sinful history because I was still wearing a mask, afraid to let others in. Thankfully, God was patient with me and allowed me to deal with these issues in my own timing. I don't think God is in a hurry like others can be with us. But, I'll admit, it's hard to have deep connections with others when we are hiding behind our masks. It's even more difficult to connect on a deeper spiritual level with the Lord when there are still layers of shame wedged between us.

Building a Family

A little over two years after having my first child , I had a healthy little girl, Marlana. She was such a beautiful miracle. I was so excited to have a little girl of my very own. It amazes me how God can multiply our love. We had so much fun together. There were hours of playing games, stories at bedtime, Sunday school, babies snuggling in our bed and in our arms. There were animals running around the house, poopy diapers, laughter, fighting, kissing away the boo- boos . . . and it all felt so "normal". I loved my life with these babies. I may not have seen my mom's eyes light up when she looked at me, but my children made my eyes and heart brighten every time I looked at them.

Around this time we moved to South California for my husband's job. Two years later, after healing from another miscarriage, I had a healthy baby boy. Micah, our third child was a bit of a challenge and kept us all on our toes, but we were happy. We were a family of five and enjoying every moment. Campfires at the beach at sunset, hikes, and bike rides filled our days. Holidays were delightful and we would go "all out" on birthday parties. How could I fall more in love than I was with my husband and with this family? My husband was such a fun dad. He used to put candy in each child's special spot in the car where he knew they sat. He would hide gifts in their room or put his day old socks under my pillow as a joke. I love the way he chased us around the house or played stupid games on us. Laughter filled our home.

The only rough patch during those years was when my youngest son was diagnosed with Blount disease. He had to wear a triangle brace from his hips down to his special made shoes. He hated them and cried a lot. We had to carry him around and that was hard because at 10 months he was already walking, but with the braces, he was being forced to stop. Micah wore the braces until he was about two years old. It was truly a blessing that he didn't need surgery. We praised God for that miracle.

I did get pregnant once more but began to lose the baby. I was too far along to let the miscarriage happen naturally, so I went to the hospital for the procedure. It was Easter night. It was much too painful to continue going through this, and I was having too many female problems. The doctors recommended sterilization and I agreed to have the surgery. *In heaven I will be surrounded by "all" my children and then we will be complete as a family.*

I can't think of a better way to end this chapter than to look at scripture and hear the voice of David in Psalm 103. David knew that God had rescued him from the pit and that he had been touched and crowned in forgiveness and loving kindness which is so healing to the soul. I've also experienced freedom from a pit or two!

Psalm 103

Bless the Lord, O my soul; and all this is within me, bless His holy name! Bless the Lord O my soul and forget not all His benefits. Who forgives all your iniquities, who heals all your diseases, Who redeems your life from destruction, who crowns you with loving kindness and tender mercies. Who satisfies your mouth with good things, so that your youth is renewed like the eagles. The Lord executes righteousness and justice for all who are oppressed. He made known His ways to Moses, His acts to the children of Israel. The Lord is merciful and gracious, slow to anger, and bounding in mercy. He will not always strive with us, nor will He keep His anger forever. He has not dealt with us according to our sins, nor punished us according to our iniquities. For as the heavens are high above the earth, so great is His mercy toward those who fear Him; as far as the east is from the west, so far has He removed our transgressions from us. As a father pities his children, so the Lord pities those who fear Him. For He knows our frame; He remembers that we are dust. As for man, his days are like grass; as a flower of the field, so he flourishes. For the wind passes over it, and it is gone, and its place remembers it no more. But the mercy of the Lord is from everlasting to everlasting on those who fear Him, and His righteousness to children's children, to such as keep His covenant, and to those who remember His commandments to do them. The Lord has established His thrown in heaven, and His kingdom rules over all. Bless the Lord, you His angels, who excel in strength, who do His word, heeding the voice of His word. Bless the Lord, all you His hosts, you ministers of His, who do His pleasure. Bless the Lord, all His works, in all places of His dominion. Bless the Lord, O my soul!

Are you finding yourself in a difficult test today? Are you feeling pressed in? Have you fallen into a pit time and time again? The Lord knows our frame, and He redeems us from all destruction. Call out your need to Jesus, remembering that His mercy is new every day.

God Always Knew

Deep Called Out to Deep

*There is a place within my soul that God's Spirit alone can hear
the silent cries of unspoken wounds.
It is only His eyes that can penetrate into the deep well
and secret recesses of my heart and
know the whirlpool of need I have.*

*Deep has called out to deep...
and there unfolds a genuine intimacy with my Maker.
I am overcome by His grace...for He takes hold of the voids and
restores them; then establishes me to stand strong in His will
and be still in my faith, knowing. . . that He is God.
And it is in that knowledge . . . the significance of the worth
and weight of the truth of Him, that I can go on.*

~~~

*Simple Blessings
K.M.*

5

Deep Calls Out To Deep

*I*n the book of Psalm, David cries, "deep call out to deep". There are some places within our soul that truly only the Lord can share in. He alone can go into that deep pool of pain —areas we must invite Him into, past our layers of protection. For we have a High Priest in Christ who experienced the things we go through and even deeper things of the soul (Heb 4:14). He carried us along—and He has carried me through!

Will You Still Love God?

In 1996 our family moved up to the state of Washington because Jim was offered a better job. We moved into a beautiful house where I was a stay-at-home mom. My life was filled with volunteering, school work, bible studies, Sunday school, vacations, sports, and taking care of my family. Who knew or could have imagined that I was made for motherhood? God knew. It was during this time that I began to thrive. I wanted to "set up a tent" (like Peter in the transfiguration of Jesus Christ) so I would never have to leave, go down that hill, and face any more difficulties.

My husband had been experiencing pain in his groin area for about a year. It was affecting his love of running which concerned him. Tests revealed that he had cancer. The salivary gland cancer he'd had in his mouth before we married had metastasized to his pelvic bone and lungs. He was 47 years old.

Of course, the diagnosis was devastating to us. It was as if the air had been sucked from our lungs. For a day or so we were in shock, but then we shifted to panic mode as we frantically researched our options and prayed fervently out of our desperation. We refused to let the disease take us down. We were confident that we could take control of this "cancer thing", secure in our belief that all our efforts would bring about healing. After all, weren't we walking the Christian road? How could there not be a miraculous healing? Isn't that how it is supposed to work? We assumed God would *only* want to heal on this side of heaven to give Him the best glory. We had not surrendered to His will for our lives, yet. We didn't know we were about to face a test that would ask us if we would still be faithful to God if what we loved was taken away. We would (we all would as a family) enter into a season of great trial. Would I collapse in despair and make more layers, or would I allow myself to be enlarged by the trial and permit others to enter into my pain? Would I walk in victory or would more layers wrap around my heart to protect against the pain? That is what every trial will ask of each of us. How will we answer when our test comes?

Sweet Surrender

My husband spent the next six years being treated by every cocktail of chemo they could mix and experiment on him, as well as the firing of radiation into his lungs. He had innumerable lab draws; X-rays, MRI's, CAT scans, PET scans, surgery and many hospitalizations. I wonder how many know the mouse on the wheel in the cage of the cancer patient. The cancer that had gone to his lungs never shrank or disappeared. We would not have our miracle of healing this side of heaven.

Jim never complained or raised his fist at God during all of this. He tried to be as normal and "unsick" as he could for his kids (always thinking of others). He continued to work and be a part of our children's lives with school and sports. Some evenings, we would all just gather on our bed and play cards, betting with pennies enjoying the laughter and teasing.

I doubt if anyone who saw him attend church during his illness ever knew what it took to get him there. I would put him in the wheelchair from the side of the bed and then wheel him to the top of our stairs. Next, I would get him out and help him sit on the top step (while holding his oxygen bottle). He would slowly and painfully go down all 15 stairs on his bottom. Then, I would rush up to grab his wheelchair and carry it down and again place him back in the chair and then attempt to put him in the car. Of course, upon returning home we would go through the whole process all over again. For those who take for granted their choice to show up or sleep in on a Sunday, I'd like to make a bold statement on behalf of my Jim. It cost him so much energy and pain to have the privilege to worship our Lord on His day with fellow believers and drink in the message from our pastor. Some of you know this routine because you may have a special needs child or person with the same medical condition. My heart goes out to you, and I understand your exhaustion.

I watched this beautiful strong 6'4" man whose arms could wrap around me, giving me the safety he knew I needed, become a man of bones with skin limply safeguarding them. Even in his frail condition, Jim could still light up my eyes and make my heart beat just a bit faster with delight. There is a love that goes so deep that words seem impossible to express it. I believe it is what the Lord would want for every married couple, to truly become one.

I remember one especially tender moment that Jim and I shared. I had been complaining one evening that my feet were sore. Jim was barely able to walk or even breathe without difficulty around this time, yet he was still the kindest of gentlemen. I watched him slowing and strenuously get out of bed to make his way to the bathroom. Never in a million years could I imagine what he was attempting (I would have refused his kindness). He returned with some lotion and painfully came to the side of the bed and rubbed my feet with his crippled hands and broken body. I witnessed and enjoyed probably the most unselfish act in all my life. My husband taught me to live like the Lord would have us live by the way he faced his death. To say that my husband was stoic is truly an understatement.

He quietly endured the pain and hospital times without drama and without seeking attention for himself. I wonder how deep His faith and personal fellowship with Jesus had to be for him to respond the way he did. He didn't even ask for help, until it became obvious that the cancer had invaded his ability to walk, breathe on his own, eat solid food, and eventually taking his voice away. But, cancer could not take or touch our love—that grew even more.

Jim decided that he didn't want to die in a hospital but wanted to spend his last days in our home. Gosh, that was an incredibly difficult discussion to have with the love of my life. I was able to honor his request, though at times I was totally overwhelmed as the sole caregiver. It was a privilege to care for him, clean him and caress this great love of mine. Even sweeter, he was able to receive that from me.

My husband's dignity was preserved in spite of having a disease that tried to steal it away. Caring for him was a gift I was given and was able to give back to him. Not all gifts are fun, easy or wrapped in shiny ribbons… some gifts are painful, but necessary for our growth. It was a painful gift to help my husband accept his own death and to help him release this world. I hope my children can give me that help when the time comes. We gave him much comfort by letting him know that although we'd miss him forever, we'd be okay. At times, it was pretty unbearable to see the daily pain in my children as they lived in grief, when it should have been a time of carefree teenage years. Grief can change a person's personality, and I pray that each of us can grow and be better because we lived in and through such an experience.

Our oldest child Brenden was luckiest to have his daddy for two extra years before the "rest came". As the oldest, I believe he may have absorbed the pain at the hardest time of one's life. Brenden was 11 years old when his dad first got sick and 17 years old when his daddy died. Pain still lives so deep within his heart that I can only pray one day he will unearth it and will be able to use his "gift of words" that God has given him to voice the ache.

Our daughter Marlana was the typical daddy's little girl. Daddy was her North Star. Her night sky is a bit darker since her daddy has left her world. She was 10 in the beginning of his illness and 16 when he died.

My Husband

I Miss . . .

~The way he would rub his scratchy feet on my legs in bed at night knowing I would squeal out in disgust.
~The way he always kept his hand on my back or leg while we slept.
~How he would cross a room with eyes only for me.
~Resting my head on his chest, listening to his heartbeat and knowing I was always safe in his arms.
~How he made everyone's birthday so special.
~His humor . . . his laughter . . . the way he loved me.
~I miss our fights ('cuz we had them).
~I miss his love letters. (Oh, how I miss his love letters.)

I Loved . . .

~The way we prayed by bedside together.
~The way he loved each of his children for who they were and trusted in who they will become.
~How he never blamed what others had done to him out of their own prejudice.

I Admired . . .

~His loyalty, integrity, and dependability.
~His unselfishness by placing Christ first in his life, then me, then his children.
~His intelligence.

I miss my best friend, my lover, the father of my children—I miss my husband.

Every girl needs her daddy to help her see that she shines as a "true jewel" in his own eyes and in the eyes of the Lord. I try to encourage her to call on her Heavenly Father now for truth.

My youngest child Micah was so in love with his daddy, in fact, he "made us" place a mattress next to our bed so he could take care of his dad's needs toward the end of his life. I believe he also wanted to watch to make sure his dad's chest would rise with one more precious breath. Micah was 6 years old when is dad first got diagnosed and 12 when his dad passed on to heaven. How could this not change a little person's personality?

Sorrow hovered in our home, never far from any of us. It's crazy to try to live "normally" when nothing is normal! At one particular doctor's appointment, we were told of two horrific ways that Jim would experience his own death. We left there numb, not saying a word, not even looking at one another. After dropping him off at home, I then picked up my son to take him to his baseball game. I sat in those bleachers, surrounded by parents joyfully shouting at the excitement of the game, silently thinking about what we had just been told and wondering what we were about to experience as a family. How surreal . . . how insane . . . how not normal! But, we attempted to put on a "good face" and tried to help others not be uncomfortable with our reality. This is a tough position to be in. I found that most people don't want to enter into that kind of sorrow and seem to just want to know that you are "okay".

I have learned much in my years of walking through the valley of the shadow death. God's Word became life to me then and certainly to my husband also. They were a sweet melody to his heart and brought him great comfort, as did our pastor when he'd come by to play softly on his guitar by my husband's bedside. I can only pray I am given that compassion when my time comes. What an unselfish gift my pastor gave to be willing to enter into our sadness.

No more would I see my Bible reading as a choice to pick up or do without. It was the only light that shined through in the dark and messy haze of grief. Some days I wanted to just scream as I watched people going about their own business seemingly so carefree. Of course, I didn't know if they were going through difficult stuff also. At the time, I was just feeling my own painful mess. How could anyone have known how deeply our hearts were breaking? .Even as we move forward today, grief is a part of the fabric of our days. Not a in a bad way, but in a way that keeps my heart tender toward others.

As I end this chapter, I share Psalm 77 as a reminder to me of when I cried out to the Lord just as Asaph (choir director to King David and contributing writer of the Psalms) because I saw my need for Him. He gave ear to me, and carried me in my overwhelmed state.

Psalms 77

I cried out to God with my voice—to God with my voice; And He gave ear to me. In the day of my trouble I sought the Lord; my hand was stretched out in the night without ceasing; my soul refused to be comforted. I remembered God, and was troubled; I complained, and my spirit was overwhelmed. Selah

You hold my eyelids open; I am so troubled that I cannot speak. I have considered the days of old, the years of ancient times. I call to remembrance my song in the night; I meditate within my heart, and my spirit makes diligent search. Will the Lord cast off forever? And will He be favorable no more? Has His mercy ceased forever? Has His promise failed forevermore? Has God forgotten to be gracious? Has He in anger shut up His tender mercies? Selah

And I said, "This is my anguish; but I will remember the years of the right hand of the Most High." I will remember the works of the LORD; surely I will remember Your wonders of old. I will also meditate on all Your work,
And talk of Your deeds. Your way, O God, is in the sanctuary; Who is so great a God as our God? You are the God who does wonders; You have declared Your strength among the peoples.

You have with Your arm redeemed Your people, the sons of Jacob and Joseph. Selah

The waters saw You, O God; the waters saw You, they were afraid; the depths also trembled. the clouds poured out water; the skies sent out a sound; Your arrows also flashed about. The voice of Your thunder was in the whirlwind; the lightnings lit up the world; the earth trembled and shook. Your way was in the sea, Your path in the great waters, and Your footsteps were not known. You led Your people like a flock by the hand of Moses and Aaron.

Do you need to hear God's voice today? The Lord's presence is our medicine for any brokenness we are dealing with. Cry out now, to Him. He hears you! _____

SO WORTHY

*When the demands of life seem to contend
and even weaken our faith—
we know to stand strong on the rock of Your promises...
for You are sure, unshakeable, and so worthy to be praised.*

*In times of questioning the plans of life
set before us—
we know to cast ourselves into the deep waters of Your promises...
for You are refreshing, patient, and so worthy to be trusted.*

*Through the moments that we lack the courage
to even move forward—
we know to take flight in the power within the spread of Your wings...
for You are strong, mighty, and so worthy in making our hope soar.*

*Oh Lord, take our cares, fears, and weakness
into Your extended, steadfast and awaiting hands—
recall to us that we may always find rest in Your tender love...
so that we might walk out in the authority of our birthright
which You have given to each of us.*

~~~

*Simple Blessings
K.M.*

God Always Knew

6

Saying Our Good-Byes

In February 2002, I can honestly say that since I was my husband's only caregiver, his illness took all my focus. He had not wanted people in our home and did not want hospice care. I was tired. As such, my energy and attention for my children's needs were lacking during this time. Our youngest, Micah, kept having reoccurring flu-like symptoms. He had fevers, vomiting, and was lethargic. I was torn to take him to the doctor because I didn't want to leave my husband's bedside. Jim needed 24 hour care at this point. Along with the oxygen, meds, personal care, he also needed the comfort of knowing he wasn't alone in these last days, these last hours. But there was no choice. Our son was getting worse every day.

Once at the doctors, you can call it mother's intuition, but I believe God whispered in my heart to ask them for a blood test. I could only imagine low iron in his blood, never a thought that it could be cancer. We were rushed to a local hospital for more testing and then the doctors took me out to the hallway to tell me that my Micah, only 12 at the time had Leukemia— Acute Myeloid Leukemia! If my husband's diagnosis felt like the wind being taken from our lungs, this felt more like the crush of our hearts. Can a heart stop beating and one still survive? Every part of me was dissolving away with the acid-like pain. I was at the end of myself. At the same time, God was soothing layers of His anointing oil onto me and into each of those deep hidden places.

The doctors said he needed to be taken immediately to Seattle's

Children's Hospital. I just couldn't process those words that seemed to be twirling in my head. The hallway walls became enormous, almost pressing into us from both sides—a blinding massive white. The world stopped for a moment. It was as though I had an out of body experience, and was watching from above. Finally coming back to my senses, I simply screamed to them that this was impossible and that my own husband was dying. Didn't they know this doesn't happen twice to a family?

Walking back into my son's hospital room and seeing him laying in the bed so very pale and sick, and knowing that I must tell my own child he had cancer, was the cruelest and most difficult moment in my life. We wept and cried and held on to each other that night. I knew the fear that pulsed in my own head (like a strobe light going off with my own private thoughts). I can't begin to imagine his fear because by then, we were familiar with what cancer does to a person and a family.

Some things you just do on almost auto pilot when you're in shock. Late in the evening we were released to drive in the Northwest's horrible mid-winter conditions, across the bridge toward Seattle's Children's hospital. Simply put . . . INSANE! Was it God's angels that steered my car for me and kept the other cars far from my own? Between my poor night vision; the welling up of tears, and trying to calm my son and myself while driving in an area I had never been in before, this was not only dangerous but ludicrous! No one in that hospital should have sent us out in those conditions. I was not thinking clearly, for sure!

My next horrible assignment that night came when I had to call home to tell my other children and my husband the terrible report. Having to give news like that over the phone and not be able to weep together and hold on to one another goes against everything a mother and wife naturally feels. It just seemed so wrong.

That first night in the emergency room many friends and my pastor Robert Case showed up. Did I call them? I don't remember. But they came in the spirit of Gods' love and poured it out onto us with words of hope and strength. Roman 12:15 & 16 says for us to weep with those that weep and to be of the same mind toward one another. Without hope, we cannot live, and I needed them to bring me that reminder. God has been so good to us and we must remember His goodness. *That is what will get us out of bed each day.*

Testing was done that night to see what kind of Leukemia Micah had. It would be days until we would know. We were taken up to the 3rd floor (the cancer ward) and to our new room to settle in for what would be our home away from home for the next nine months as long as he didn't develop any side effects that would delay our release and his treatment. But, we'd soon find out that my son would develop every possible side effect and our stay would last almost a year and half with a few weeks between to come home and regain strength before more chemo. I have no words that could ever express how I feel about the treatment we have today to fight cancer. Some things are better left unsaid. Just the thought of even taking my child to stay in a hospital was difficult enough, but then to see the "cancer ward" sign was just another harsh reminder of our current reality.

The next few days were a whirlwind of learning our new routine as a hospital patient, meeting our different doctors, and learning what their titles meant to us. I received and made a million phone calls keeping everyone up to date on what was happening and asking for help with the care of my husband and kids. The hardest part of all for me was being asked to sign the papers to put the many cocktails of poison in my baby to kill the good and bad cells in his body. We'd then have to *hope and pray* that the treatment didn't kill him. I signed my name to that agreement, but it was a very surreal moment for me, and I'm sure for many other parents.

My new daily routine included waking up every morning at 5 am in order to drive home to see my other two children off to school and then have time with my husband. I called my husband's wonderful sister, Linda, to come and help care for him while I was with my son. She unselfishly came. I only had those few hours in the early morning with him. I felt I was needed more with my son. A hospital is a frightening place for any child but even more so if that child has cancer.

When it comes to family, one should never have to choose where your loyalty lies, but I had to make that choice every day. Do I spend time with the man who was my whole world, my greatest love? He was living in excruciating pain and could barely breathe anymore. He only had days and/or moments left. Or, do I choose my baby who needed his mother by his side as the cancer invaded his body.? He was being pumped with chemo that was making him sicker with each hour. Can a heart stop beating and you survive? There will never be a "right" answer for me, and I will carry my choices with me always. Even today, right now, this decision leaves an ache within my soul that only God can touch and heal.

Seattle's Children's Hospital was so amazingly compassionate toward us. They offered to have an ambulance pick up my husband and transport him to my son's room where he could be hooked up to the oxygen in the room. That way they could be together. But it was just too much, too overwhelming for my husband's delicate state. The hospital staff then went the extra mile to cut through red tape so that we could go home for a visit instead. It's against hospital policy for a child to leave once he or she begins treatment because their blood counts are compromised, but they made the exception for us. They masked up his face, body and hands, and then sent us out with only a three hour window to take in a home visit. I wheeled my son to the car and we drove back home to have his (and what would be mine also) very last and very precious hours with Jim. We now hold on to this bittersweet moment and will for the rest of our lives. I thank the Lord above who arranged the tenderness in those doctors' hearts, to enable them to bend the rules and allow us to have our last time, our last memory, and our last good-byes.

If anyone has done one of those "bedside vigils" you know what a gift it is to be able to say your thank-you's and your good-byes. I think the sounds coming from our mouths are more of a muttering through the onslaught of tears as we're forced to push formulated words pass that darn lump in our throat. But no matter how poorly those words are said, there is comfort in knowing you had that chance. Many of you have experienced such bitter sweetness.

There we stood by the upstairs bed, a place where much love had been given freely to one another throughout the years. And now this place had become the dying bed. We stood shoulder to shoulder over my husband; over a daddy, over a brother, over a great man, and said our good -byes. My daughter was at a church winter retreat and never got to say her good-byes. *I have to wonder what kind of effect that must carry on her heart today.*

Just as in past times when I have wanted to "set my tent" on the mountain top, once again, I wanted to set up my tent in this valley of the shadow of death. Truth be told, I am a selfish creature and to live in the sorrow and pain with my husband was more desirable to me than the thought of having to live without him. Even knowing he would be set free from pain and be free with Jesus, I still wished I had more time with him. Even today, nine years later, if I am truly honest, on my hard days of missing him, I am still that selfish person who would choose our last few months we had together over living without him. I understand that my husband might have a different perspective now that he is alive and living with his new non-cor- ruptible body in heaven. But, I am only his widow living this side of heaven who would just want one more day with him, knowing full well that one more day would never be enough. I want to tell him all that he taught me and all that the Lord has been showing me these days. I have grown so much spiritually. I want to touch him one more time. I want to be held by him… just once more.

I write this truth today through the tears which fall from my eyes and land gently on my legal pad. I wipe them away, so I can see my words. Many a Kleenex have I gone through while writing about this time of our lives, this walk down memory lane. My layers have been peeled away, and I am now able to share my honest thoughts and feeling without the fear of someone's opinion of me. That is the work of the Holy Spirit and for me also a part of just getting older. I don't think I will ever be able to keep another layer between me and the Lord, or me and others. I'm done with that. I welcome God's Word to penetrate my heart. Hebrews 4:12 states that His Word does the work of a two-edged sword that penetrates between the soul/spirit and joint/marrow to discern between our thoughts and the intent of our heart. Bring it on Lord, for I desire to be all yours, and so I know I must allow your work in me. I welcome you.

The Silent Voice of Grief

There are moments in grief when it seems as though your emotions bear down upon your soul with the same intensity and strength of crashing waves against the ocean shorelines. Waves of unscheduled grief wash in and over your day with an unbearable pain rooted in the ripple effects of loss.

For some of us who already have a loved one waiting for us in heaven (maybe a child, mate, parent, sibling, or friend), it's not uncommon to find ourselves reaching out for a favorite framed picture of that person. In soulful anguish, we begin to carry on a one-sided conversation with that photograph as though the fervency behind our words will bring our loved one back. Does this sound strange? For those reeling from the horrific emotional battle of losing a loved one, it is not. While we're thankful for the lasting momento that we clutch against our chest, our memories are so vivid and alive that they begin to overshadow the momentary glimpse of solace that they might hold.

As we taste each fallen tear that streams down our cheek, we sometimes squeeze the picture so tightly that for a moment we believe that the strength of our ache can revive our loved one. When that doesn't happen, we fall into bed exhausted, too emotionally drained to do anything but curl up in a ball and wait . . . empty, unsatisfied, and not ready to let go. We offer our heartache up to the Lord.

I go and prepare a place for you, I will come again and receive you to Myself, that where I am there you may be also.

-John 14:3

We are sojourners, here only for a moment. We were never

meant to say good-bye to our loved ones, but since the fall of creation, that is what we must do over and over again. Jesus is preparing our "forever home" where we'll no longer have to experience the pain of our loss. While we may feel sadness now, we must remember that it's only temporary.

The apostles didn't understand what Jesus meant when He told them that he had to leave them and that He was preparing their "real home" (eternal home). Like the apostles, we have a hard time understanding why our loved ones have to leave us and why we have to wait to join them. Our heavenly home is being made especially for us. How can our imaginations even begin to picture what it will look or be like? It is that dark cloudy glass we are looking through now that scripture talks about. Yet one day, we will see Christ face to face and will understand so much more. But for now, we've been given The Comforter to strengthen, comfort and to help us understand our purpose in our pain. God draws us to Himself and nourishes our wounds with a healing balm so that we may minister that same hope to others in their time of grief. We don't even have to be "out of grief" to help others in theirs. What a privilege it is to be used in such a way until our Bridegroom comes for each us to take us home.

Lord, our pain is real and You know it so well. Thank you for Your patience and gentleness. You never dismiss or minimize our hurt. You suffered more than we could ever imagine, and You did that for us! Help us to be real with our grief, and help us to keep our eyes on the Prize (You), always walking alongside someone else with the same patience, grace and love You have shown us.

God Always Knew

Psalm 130 speaks of God's mercy and our desire to be with the Lord. I too have waited on Him as did the psalmist. My soul waits.

Psalm 130
(A song of ascents)

Out of the depths I have cried to You, O LORD; Lord, hear my voice! Let Your ears be attentive to the voice of my supplications. If You, LORD, should mark iniquities, O Lord, who could stand? But there is forgiveness with You, that You may be feared. I wait for the LORD, my soul waits, and in His word I do hope. My soul waits for the Lord more than those who watch for the morning—yes, more than those who watch for the morning. O Israel, hope in the LORD; for with the LORD there is mercy, and with Him is abundant redemption. And He shall redeem Israel from all his iniquities.

Is your soul waiting for God? He is there with you now. Stop, slow down, and wait on His still small voice that speaks into your spirit. There is much to learn in the dark place where you feel so pressed. You will learn about yourself, and more importantly, you will learn more of God's mercy for you. Let Him strengthen you now. Praise His name for His goodness.

The Warmth of Your Blanket

I clutched your blanket until late into the night hoping to experience some kind of closeness to you, but only my tears fall freely as I allowed myself the time and indulgence of truly missing you.

Your blanket once wrapped gingerly across your thinning frame as death continued to overtake your body; now it lays empty as a stark reminder you are no longer here beside me.

Oh how I spent the night grappling and crying out to the Lord for His mercy to help me endure this heart ache; and still yet this soft material is without you in it.

Finally weary and overcome with exhaustion, I lay under the covering of your blanket and Christ sweetly reminded me that He is and has always been my covering. The closeness I want; the tears that fall; the time given over and heartache felt…are all mine to choose to surrender into His loving care—and so I do.

Now your blanket seems to radiate new warmth with remembering the comfort of having God's presence with me; and as I drift off to sleep, I know it will only be my dreams that will take me once again to you.

~~~

Simple Blessings
K.M.

God Always Knew

7

Grace For The Journey

My son and I were alone in our private thoughts as we quietly traveled back to the hospital. After we got situated in our room and a few hours had passed, the phone rang and seemed to breach the silent atmosphere of our room. It was my sister-in-law telling me that our Jim was gone now. He had left "his earthly tent", laid it down, and was being welcomed into heaven and into the arms of Jesus.

My oldest son, Brenden, was with his father in his last moments. How I wish I was also there to be able to lay softly by his side and kiss away his last breath. I wish it was me and not my son that witnessed the gentlemen from the funeral home place his daddy in the black plastic bag and carry him away and out of his life forever. How sobering that pain must be. Yet, God has a road for each of us to travel and that hard one was for my sweet son to travel and experience. Hebrews 13:5 lets us know that God will never leave us or forsake us. We must remember this as we go along on "our special" assignments. We have the promise of His presence and *that* must be our comfort.

My youngest son and I had our own road to travel. The next day following the death of my husband, my daughter arrived home only to be told about her daddy's passing. She too must face her own road of grief. I was glad that on that first night of her arrival, the staff at the hospital turned a blind eye and allowed her to stay in our hospital room on this very difficult first night of grief. We just clung together with exhausting sorrow.

Tears

During our son's stay at the hospital, tears flowed easily from my eyes. I could not hold back the reservoir of emotions that was building up within me. Tears are God's gifts to us — a special language of the heart. My son and children saw many tears fall, and we all understood this healing language more deeply than words could ever express.

One afternoon at Children's Hospital, I went upstairs to the parent's bathroom where parents of sick kids could go and freshen up or to be alone. I needed to drown out the inward screams of unfairness; to cry uncontrollably and allow the shower water to mix and carry away the flow of tears. I was praying, crying out, begging God to see us, to hear me, to help us. Did He not know I was at the end of my rope, my coping skills, my sanity? My heart hurt, and it seemed more than I could bare. I reminded Him of His Word. He promised to not allow more than we could handle, and I did not think I could handle any more. I was done.

Have you pleaded with the Lord, begged Him cried out for mercy? I am not ashamed to boldly cry on the name of Jesus!

After the exhausting work of pouring out my painful weary heart to the Lord, I gathered myself together and headed back to Micah's room. As I was getting off the elevator, the Lord filled my heart with the verse from John 9:4. (paraphrase) "We must work quickly to carry out the task that has been given, for the time is short and night is almost here." I instantly knew He was letting me know, that through this tragedy, this ache, He was going to display His work through us (John 9:3). "How Lord? " I asked, "Who am I? He then reminded me that regardless of my background, I knew Him, and that's all that mattered. He chooses whom He will work through so that His name alone will be glorified. He was telling me that through my weakness others would see His power.

This was the day I became fully engaged in God's work, and the day the Lord lanched me out of my comfort zone, out of my circumstances, and out into the world to be a bold witness for Him. He used this trial —the trial so many people were watching us go through— to enlarge His Kingdom. As newspaper reporters and the local TV reporters came out for interviews, or as my many emails were forwarded on for prayers, I began to understand that this was our time to stand boldly on the promises God had given us. And, although we'd walked through the valley of the shawdow of death, we had a peace inside that could only point to Jesus. This was the light that God wanted us to carry for the world to see. His light.

Still today, I have never lost that fire which He placed in me. I am still moving forward and speaking out unashamedly about what He's done for me in my life. I've learned that whatever God sees fit to allow into our lives (the good and the difficult), if it is what He chooses to use in order to bring more people into the Kingdom, or to encourage a weary believer, or to enlarge my own faith... then none of it will ever be in vain.

Our "why's" (why did this happen to ME) only limit our perspective as we attempt to place God in an imaginary box, while our "what's" (Lord, what will you do to bring good out of this?) release us to activate our faith and accept God's Will.

In the days and months that followed, it felt (and was) so very wrong to be separated from my other two children in their grief over their daddy's death and fear for their brother's life. I am their mother, and I should have been able to wrap my arms around them in the night as each one would cry out for their loss. Although this is an ache within me today, it is also a pain I must continually hand over to the Lord. I will not allow the beginnings of any more layers to keep me from intimacy with my God by letting anger or bitterness or even sadness control me.

Within a few days after Jim's passing, we had his memorial service. My mother-in-law flew up for it and my sister-in-law stayed for it. What a pitiful sight we must have been. There we all sat in the front row wishing we could be anywhere but there. Each of my children was so lost in the heaviness of sorrow. They sat, lined up in their chairs, greeting others, being polite, but all the while wanting to scream out the silent ache just churning inside them. I am sure they wished they could run out and escape the madness. This "time honored ritual" we do as a society seems so absurd to walk through when it is your turn personally!

To add to the bewilderment of the scene playing out before us, Micah also sat there all gloved and masked in hospital attire at his daddy's memorial. The doctors wanted Micah to avoid any harmful germs from others because he had begun his chemo. It was such a pitiful site to behold and yet such a blessing that he could be there.

An Outpouring of Love

Ephesians says for us to bear one another's burden, and so many did just that! It was like a mini whirlwind. I am still unaware of just how many people stepped up to walk us through this very stressful and sorrowful time. I received flowers, neighbors held car washes and golf tournaments to raise money for us. People cleaned my home; folded my laundry, made meals, did back breaking yard work, painted my bedroom and gave it a fresh new look. We even had a young couple come out and stay at our place for a short time to be there for my older children while Micah and I were in the hospital.

We received notes of support and gift cards as well as Sunday school and public school encouragements.

The outpouring of compassion onto our little hurting family helped move us forward as we dealt with not only the death of the head of our home and the center of our hearts, but also the unbearable possibility of death for the youngest member of our family. How could we ever thank people enough who ventured into that kind of mess? I must trust that God Himself will shower each of them with the riches of His pleasure.

Moving Forward

Micah and I spent most of the next year in Children's Hospital as a requirement for his Leukemia treatment. My daughter Marlana was finishing up 9th grade and my son Brenden was finishing up his senior year. It was hard to not be involved very much during my two children's graduating years. Being away from home and caring so intensely for Micah left little of me to give. I often wonder if they know how deeply it pained me to be away from them during such a critical time. I also wonder what affect that has had on them, even today? *While it may be true that children are resilient (so the saying goes), sorrow runs deep, and can follow us into our adulthood. We must not assume that our children are "doing fine" just because they never mention their pain or they seem to be "handling it".*

After a year of treatment for Micah came another year and a half of trying to bring my son back to life. It was a long and drawn out hard road. Micah developed every side effect from the chemo treatments. He developed a skin infection that they thought might be the dreaded "flesh eating disease", but it wasn't. Then, a fungus started to grow and take over his lungs. Lung surgery removed the dangerous fungus, but then he got pericarditis (fluid around the heart) which is very dangerous and painful. The outside walls of his lungs expanded due to the irritation caused by one of the chemo treatments. They expanded so much that they pressed against themselves and caused incredible pain. That same chemo made his eyes go blind for about a week. Shingles, pneumonia, high fevers, osteopenia (which lead to many bone breaks) were some of the other side effects that he endured. He continued with low blood counts for years needing blood transfusions, platelets, and a daily shot of GCSF to help him with his low white blood count. And yet, I never heard or saw my boy give up hope . . . but I did. One day in particular, I was home trying to gather more clothes for us. I laid down on my bedroom carpet and cried like a child, protesting this cruelty. I wept for my pain and for my son's pain. I asked God to take him—take my son to heaven to be with his daddy. I couldn't be selfish and allow him to stay here in this kind of physical pain. I couldn't watch him go through this agony anymore. I truly trusted in God's love. I knew His love was bigger than mine, and He loved my son more than I could ever hope to. I laid my boy down on the altar.

God had something else in His plan. Micah had been prayed over by our pastors and elders. They laid hands upon him and stood in unity with the healing God was going to do. He had my son's life in His hands. Now was the time to wait to see what kind of journey we would be asked to take. My husband was also anointed and prayed over, but it was God's choice to bring him home to heaven. We are still learning to journey through what has been asked of all of us, knowing God equips us to do that with His grace!

Time passed slowly. Micah went from a wheelchair (hooked up to medicine and liquid food), to walking on his own. Then, he went back to school. Even more amazing was when Micah grew strong enough to join the basketball team and play throughout his high school year! I watched him go on mission trips to Germany and to an orphanage in Bulgaria with his older brother so he could help the children there. The power of God is something to behold. I stand in humble amazement at such a power.

Around this time I received word my mother had passed away from cancer. She never called or asked me to help. Like my father, she never left me a note or any last comforting words. She died never wanting any kind of relationship with me or my family. The sting of that still hurts today, but I am reminded that this is just another loss to give to the Lord for Him to heal.

The Rose

If I could give a picture of what my journey of healing from a painful past looks like, it would be that of a firmly closed, yet tender rose bud. Life exposed the tender root of my soul to harsh elements, and just like the rose, I kept a barrier of thorns surrounding me. But, that is never God's plan.

God lovingly placed the stem of my tender heart into His enriched soil of repentance and forgiveness. Under the warmth of the Son's love and the nourishment of the watering of God's Word, I began to grow. As the Holy Spirit blew gently upon my weakened petals cowering in shame, each tightly held petal began to release its tight grip until I was able to bloom fully with hope and expectancy.

Although remnants of a few thorns still remain, they have softened and are hardly even noticeable. It is my prayer that I now release a sweet smelling aroma that pleases the Gardener Himself, but also invites other passers-by to marvel at the beauty for ashes that has become my life.

God always knew I was a rose meant to be in full bloom, and He is patient with the completion of that work. As His creations, we each contain a sweet smelling fragrance that He is waiting to uncover. When we begin to trust this truth and receive His grace into our lives, healing and maturity take place. It is then that we are able to extend the beauty of God's grace to another.

Our oldest son Brenden finished his two years of college and then left to teach English in Prague for a year. He has "wanderlust"—the travel bug. He enjoys caring for the helpless and is a gentle soul. He is so very kind to this mother. I believe he will make a good husband and father one day. And he still has a smile which could light up any room!

Our daughter moved to Texas for a year and did a bit of college. She lived on her own to learn some independence before returning to Washington. She has a passion for horses and is great with dogs of all kinds. Marlana is one who will delight in being a stay-at-home rancher's wife. Got to love that! I'm thrilled by the way she makes me laugh and fills me in on what's going on in her life. I love our "girl time" and that we are slowly beginning to share our deepest pain. At the writing of this book, Micah is in his third year of college and is staying healthy.

Each of my children has their own layers of protection surrounding their hearts, but they're working on them. They don't always agree with me right now about those layers, but I battled so many myself that I can't help but share what I've learned. I can see how each one holds back with their emotions, maybe choosing not to go that deep (at least with me). I've accepted that it may be too difficult to talk with a mother who grieves for her own losses. I understand this and give them space to grow. But when they are ready, they will find God has been waiting on them. His desire is to show them His ability to carry this very heavy load for them. They will also find a mother who desperately wants to go that deep with each of them.

Lets us look upon Psalm 93 which shouts to us that God cannot be moved by *any* kind of problem. It can be a tendency within all of us to only see the difficult part of a battle—the sorrow, the pain. But, if we could also see how God pours Himself out to each of us and blesses us with His presence, we would stand amazed. Is that something you also need to do today? Can you see how God will not hold back His grace as He takes you through the journey? His is an infinite power. His name is above all and worthy of our praise.

Psalm 93

The LORD reigns, He is clothed with majesty; the LORD is clothed, He has girded Himself with strength. Surely the world is established, so that it cannot be moved. Your throne is established from of old; You are from everlasting. The floods have lifted up O LORD, the floods have lifted their voice; the floods lift up their waves. The LORD on high is mightier than the noise of many waters, than the mighty waves of the sea. Your testimonies are very sure; Holiness adorns your house, O LORD, forever.

Why do bad things happen? Will we ever really understand that question this side of heaven? To be sure, when there are difficulties, if we draw closer to the Lord, He will draw closer to mend our broken hearts. If compassion means "shared hurt", then think of how connected we can be with others who are going through a difficult time. Is God calling you to walk alongside someone to be an encourager? Share your thoughts with Him. _____

God Always Knew

How Will I Know

*How will I know if I am a woman of trust until tested by life's
heaviness pressing and crushing in, and yet…
I discover You my God, are here with strong hands extended
waiting to take my hand in Yours.*

*How will I know if I am a woman of faith until what I've tightly held
is stripped and taken away, and yet…
it is just that which allows me
to behold Your beauty as my one thing I desire.*

*How will I know if I am a woman of hope until discouragement and
loneliness creep in, and yet…
I've encountered that my alone time
spent and given over to You Lord, satisfies completely.*

*How will I know if I am a woman of forgiveness until being wronged
and tested with unfairness, and yet…
when asked, I learn to surrender the pain
over and into Your care.*

*How will I know if I am a woman of joy—filled praise until what I
loved so dearly has gone from my life and yet…
the dependency on You has produced a song of worship in my heart
for my Savior who never leaves me.*

*And finally, how do I know if I am a woman of love until these
hardships are allowed to transform me into Your image, Jesus, so I
can see the world and touch it with the heart like Yours.*

~~~

*Simple Blessings
K.M.*

8

Hope and a Future

Have you ever heard anyone say, "Do not despise where God has you, even if it is in a desert"? For me, this is an undeniably true statement. Doesn't it tell us in Luke 5:16 that Christ went into the wilderness to pray? And don't we do our most direct, simple, and earnest prayers in the hard places? The Lord draws us to Himself in those tight places and speaks softly to us with His loving words. But frequently, it takes being lifted from that hard place to be able to look back in retrospect to grasp some understanding of the fruit that developed from that experience.

The Lord helped me to understand this essential truth after years of struggling to get a grip on my many moods of sorrow that I faced after the loss of my husband. As I sought God for comfort, He began to show me that during my marriage, I'd become dependent on Jim to "rescue" me from my emotional struggles with my past instead of relying on God, the Ultimate Healer. So, when my "cheerleader" Jim was no longer in my life—the pits were mine to face (not alone) with God's help. It has been hard work. I have wrestled mightily with this new revelation and have come to understand that depending on another person to lift our heavy hearts can be an unhealthy coping mechanism. God wants us to turn to Him in our time of grief and see past the hazy film of sorrow that often keeps us focusing on our pain instead of God's love and will for our life.

God doesn't always explain the hard situations we must endure while here on earth—He just demands that we have faith in Him. Truthfully, most of us would rather find relief or be delivered out from trials and difficulties rather than go through the process. This is why our valleys seem to be such an interruption and violation to us. Understand that God is more interested in our sanctification through the trial rather than our deliverance from the trial itself. Pruning is never pleasant, but the fruit and beauty that will come out of it, is not only extraordinary, but useful.

My "desert time" was our year and a half at Children's Hospital. It was a desert experience even though there was no scorching sun beating down on our backs or hot sand under our feet. Nevertheless, it was heavy and filled with grief. We spent days in our hospital room with the lights turned off; T. V. and phone unplugged; window curtains pulled shut to keep out the light or any unwanted visitor while Micah dealt with excruciating pain and mounting waves of nausea.

As my son lay in bed for countless hours trying to escape the pain by forging into the quiet rest that only a deep sleep could yield him, I sat in silence with God's Holy Book in my hands. I read it cover to cover, allowing His Word to pour into my tired spirit. My time in the desert allowed me to drink of His Living Water where He would reveal Himself to me. It is there that I would learn, be refreshed, and be strengthened by Him as He nursed my wounded soul.

In John 6:68, Peter says to Jesus, "Where would we go? Your word of love gives us eternal life". I felt the same way as I hungrily devoured each precious word God was pouring into me. I was nourished in a time of uncertainty as I faced my son's unknown future. The Lord was drawing me to Him in a new way that I never understood before, and I ran straight toward Him! His presence was the light that illuminated our room with hope in a time that seemed pretty hopeless. His voice was all we needed. God was a sure and constant companion, then and now.

Does it really matter if we are married, single or widowed as long as we walk with Christ? Does it matter if we have healing on this side of heaven or on eternity's side, as long as heaven is our eternal and final home? Does it really matter if we are out in the hot desert alone; or in the city with a crowd of people, or even sitting in a dark hospital room, as long as we remain intimate with our Lord and Savior?

God doesn't always show us our future or explain His ways, and most of the time I am thankful for that. Didn't God admonish us in the book of Job, that we cannot know His ways for they are not our ways? Boy is that true! Are we to question God's authority or His goodness? He wants our simple trust, like that of a small child. He is trustworthy and worthy of our trust.

Those of us who like to hold on to our own control find this faith thing, submitting to God's will, kind of like journeying into the Wild Wild West or venturing into the last frontier. But, as the book of Hebrew tells us in the 11th chapter and 6th verse, it is our faith that pleases God.

I didn't start off well, but I can choose to end well. It is my desire most of all to please God with these last years of my life no matter what we must walk through. I say these words understanding just exactly what that might mean for each of us. These are not flippant words from someone who doesn't have a clue. I know of what I am speaking. Micah's health is so much better although he does have a lower blood count than what is on the "normal" side. We choose each day to be thankful for the health he has today. None of us are promised tomorrow, so each of us must live our lives as if Christ is coming for us today. I also know that God's love for me will never change whether I walk well or stumble along the way. His love is unmovable and unchangeable. Pretty darn amazing when you know that truth. It is very freeing.

In the years following our 2002 invasion of trauma, the four of us have continued to heal emotionally. Micah's body began to heal and he was able to get back to school after missing almost three years. I found myself with the delight and privilege of being able to teach the daytime bible study at our church. This feeds my soul. I also began to write a type of psalm–like poetry as God continues to give me much inspiration to share with others. This is a gift that has only been recently acquired that I try to honor God with. Although the enemy taunts me with my lack of education, I trust that God will continue to give me the desire to re-learn what I lost so many years ago. I am thankful, for the many dear friends God has given to me who not only support me in my writing but in other areas as well.

One day my pastor's wife invited me over to their home. It came as a big surprise to me when she asked if I would like to be the church's women ministry leader. *I accepted and remained in that position for a little over 4 years.* I never saw that coming and truly never would think myself capable. Sometimes it takes another person to see something in you that you can't even see or believe in for yourself, especially for those of us who have been beaten down by others and by ourselves. Through this new experience, God has given me a new opportunity to help heal my soul by serving the wonderful ladies in my church. He has multiplied my love in ways I never dreamed possible. It has only been through God's tender work through my mass of layers that I have been able to take part in such intimacy with my Father.

At the age of 48, I went on my first mission trip to Belize to co-teach a women's retreat. I discovered that teaching and speaking at retreats is another passion of mine. Reading and learning God's Word is something that I am passionate to share with everyone! I love dissecting God's Word and helping others with the application of the principles for our lives. I want to share what I have learned (and am still learning) with every twist and turn that comes my way. I want to encourage believers that even in the hardest and most painful times of our lives, we can trust God. We can believe in His promises for us.

Can you see how God will restore our lives in a way we could never have envisioned? I may not have been born into a supportive family, yet God gave me my husband's family and a wonderful church family. I was able to learn how to have my own healthy family. After all the years of hiding behind the layers of secrets and shame, not connecting in any deep ways with God or others, I now lead a grief support group. Who would of thought that this would ever be possible? Of course, God always knew. I now walk along others by helping them with their own family secrets, by being a good listener and not their judge. That is the work of the Holy Spirit. Only God can do that kind of work in us. I love that our church would want to have this type of support group. It allows people to be honest with their pain and losses, so that they can step out from hiding and find hope in Jesus Christ.

It has been said that a church is like a hospital taking in lots of wounded. Yet it is also a hospital's objective to send the patient back out in a healthy manner. I have seen too many churches want to sweep these true problems under a rug. It is so important to me that we can come to a safe place and share the honesty of past and present pain, then give our wounds to Jesus to heal them completely. He does. Oh, how He does!

Being alone at 50 isn't easy. I certainly never thought I would have been widowed at 43. At times I wrestle with the emotions and underlying sadness that comes with loneliness and from the distant memories of abuse. I don't want these feelings to get out of control or warp my knowledge in any way of who I am in Christ. So, I work to keep my focus on Christ alone.

There was once a time when I questioned God about the difficult roads that I've had to travel. Each lesson had been painful and puzzling to me and I wanted answers. But now, I have learned to depend on His will for my life and to be open to whatever new journey He has in store. He has revealed to me (as He has done for all of us) that we are not to settle or get cozy in our Christian walk. He knows our propensity to want to skate through life, feeling as if we have "finally made it" so that we can "retire" from our journey. This is not God's will for us, and we should never desire to be on cruise control when it comes to standing our spiritual ground in those areas that we need to fight for while here on earth. I know that trials will continue to come my way, but I've learned to see them as a privilege that God is allowing me to go through so I can know with certainty, it is God alone that I depend upon.

In Job 13:15 it says, "Yet He slay me, I will put my hope in Him..." This is no longer just an abstract thought for me, but one that I've experienced first hand. I must not settle for a life anchored in the emotions of my past, but rather choose to keep hope kindled for a future for me and my kids. I remind myself that I am not defined by my widowhood but that I am also a bride to Christ. As I keep my focus on Him, He shows me how to use my life experiences, situations, and now my singleness to help enlarge His Kingdom and strengthen believers. As His bride, I keep myself prepared in holiness for our wedding day that is yet to come. How I long for the day He returns for me, His bride-in-waiting!

Psalm 47

Oh, clap your hands, all you peoples! Shout to God with the voice of triumph! For the LORD Most High is awesome; He is a great King over all the earth. He will subdue the peoples under us, and the nations under our feet. He will choose our inheritance for us, the excellence of Jacob whom He loves. Selah

God has gone up with a shout, the LORD with the sound of a trumpet. Sing praises to God, sing praises! Sing praises to our King, sing praises! For God is the King of all the earth; sing praises with understanding. God reigns over the nations; God sits on His holy throne. The princes of the people have gathered together, the people of the God of Abraham. For the shields of the earth belong to God; He is greatly exalted.

Maybe your "beginnings" were full of turmoil and poor choices. Can you now see that God can take them, work them out, and give you hope and a future? *God always knew* for you, too. Seize this moment! Write down your hopes and dreams, but most of all your thankfulness to The One who leads you on.

_____
_____
_____
_____
_____
_____
_____
_____
_____

Author Bio

Kerry Monroe is a trained grief coach who combines her life experiences with the foundation of God's Word to walk alongside those in grief. The tragedies in her own life have deepened her compassion and empathy toward those who have experienced loss. She uses this heightened awareness to gently encourage and guide.

To find out more about Kerry Monroe and her writings, you may visit her on the web at **www.kerrymonroe.com** or email her at **GodAlwaysKnew@gmail.com**

God Always Knew

Salvation Prayer

Dear God in heaven, I come to you in the name of Jesus. I acknowledge to You that I am a sinner, and I am sorry for my sins and the life that I have lived; I need your forgiveness.

I believe that your only begotten Son Jesus Christ shed His precious blood on the cross at Calvary and died for my sins, and I am now willing to turn from my sin.

You said in Your Holy Word, Romans 10:9 that if we confess the Lord our God and believe in our hearts that God raised Jesus from the dead, we shall be saved.

Right now I confess Jesus as the Lord of my soul. With my heart, I believe that God raised Jesus from the dead. This very moment I accept Jesus Christ as my own personal Savior and according to His Word, right now I am saved.

Thank you Jesus for your unlimited grace which has saved me from my sins. I thank you Jesus that your grace never leads to license, but rather it always leads to repentance. Therefore Lord Jesus transform my life so that I may bring glory and honor to you alone and not to myself.

Thank you Jesus for dying for me and giving me eternal life.

Amen.

God Always Knew

References

I have read many books on grief, trauma, sexual abuse and healing. I've listed some of my favorites below.

Workbooks:
Recovering from the Losses of Life (Norman Wright)
Grief Share Workbook (Grief Share)
Grief Recovery Workbook (Chaplain Ray Giunta)
Redeeming The Tears: A Journey Through Grief and Loss (Serendipity House)

Books:
The Empty Chair Robert De Vries (Handling Holidays)
Experiencing Grief (Norman Wright)
The Wounded Heart (Dan Allendar) - **Excellent for sexual abuse**
Traveling Through Grief (Robert De Vries)
Crisis and Trauma Counseling (Norman Wright)
Living Fully in the Shadow of Death (Robert De Vries)
I Can't Get Over It (Aphrodite Matsakis PhD) **Good for those in PTSD**
Living With Grief After Sudden Loss: Suicide, Homicide, Accident, Heart Attack, Loss (Doka PhD)

Books to Help Children:
It's OKay to Cry (Norman Wright)
Helping Your Kids Deal with Anger, Fear and Sadness (Norman Wright)

People's Stories:
A Bend in the Road (David Jeremiah)
A Grace Disguised (Gerald Sittser)
A Grief Observed (CS Lewis)

Devotional:
Streams in the Desert (L. B. Cowman)